Sally Gal

Words and Music by Bob Dylan

Brightly

Well, I'm gon-na get you Sal - ly girl,___

I'm gon-na get you Sal - ly girl.___ I'm gon-na get you Sal - ly girl.___

(Instrumental)
I'm gon-na get you Sal - ly gal.

to Coda
I'm just one o' them

ram - blin' men, Ram - blin' since I don't___ know when. Here I come and I'm a -

D.S. al Coda
Coda
(repeat ad lib.)
gone a - gain,___ Sal - ly says___ I got no end.

(play three times)

3

When I Got Troubles

Words and Music by Bob Dylan

NO DIRECTION HOME
BOB DYLAN

A Martin Scorsese Picture

Cover design and layout by Geoff Gans
Cover photograph by Barry Feinstein

This book Copyright © 2006 Special Rider Music.
Published 2006 by Amsco Publications,
A Division of Music Sales Corporation, New York

Order No. AM 984060
International Standard Book Number: 0.8256.3452.0

Exclusive Distributors:
Music Sales Corporation
257 Park Avenue South, New York, NY 10010 USA
Music Sales Limited
8/9 Frith Street, London W1D 3JB England
Music Sales Pty. Limited
120 Rothschild Street, Rosebery, Sydney, NSW 2018, Australia

Printed in the United States of America by
Vicks Lithograph and Printing Corporation

Amsco Publications
A Part of **The Music Sales Group**
New York/London/Paris/Sydney/Copenhagen/Berlin/Tokyo/Madrid

Contents

D.C. (Instrumental) and fade

Rambler, Gambler

Traditional, arranged by Bob Dylan

once had _____ a lov - er; her age was _____ six - teen. _____ She's a flow - er _____ of _____ vel - vet and the Rose of Ce - line.

5. Her ____

Additional lyrics

2. Come sit down beside me,
   Come sit down right here.
   Come sit down, love, I want you;
   Love you boldly, so dear.

3. When you get to Wyoming,
   A letter you'll see.
   If you get into trouble,
   Just you write and tell me.

5. Her parents was against me,
   Now she is the same.
   If I writ on your book, love,
   Just you blot out my name.

6. Oh there's changes in the ocean,
   There's changes in the sea.
   There's changes in my true love;
   Ain't no change in me.

This Land is Your Land

Words and Music by Woody Gutherie

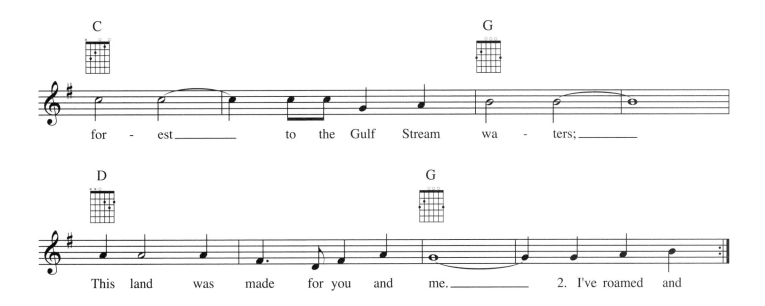

for - est_____ to the Gulf Stream wa - ters;_____

This land was made for you and me._____ 2. I've roamed and

Additional lyrics

2. I've roamed and rambled, and I've followed my footsteps
To the sparkling sands of her diamond deserts,
And all around me a voice was sounding:
This land was made for you and me.

Chorus

3. The sun comes shining as I was strolling.
The wheat fields waving and the dust clouds rolling.
The fog was lifting; a voice come chanting:
This land was made for you and me.

Chorus

4. As I was walkin', I saw a sign there,
And that sign said "No Trespassin',"
But on the other side it didn't say nothin'.
Now that side was made for you and me!

Chorus

5. In the squares of the city, in the shadow of the steeple,
Near the relief office I see my people.
And some are grumblin', and some are wonderin'
If this land's still made for you and me.

Chorus

6. Nobody living can ever stop me
As I go walking that freedom highway.
Nobody living can make me turn back;
This land was made for you and me.

Chorus

Song to Woody

Words and Music by Bob Dylan

Additional lyrics

2. Hey, hey Woody Guthrie, I wrote you a song
   'Bout a funny ol' world that's a-comin' along.
   Seems sick an' it's hungry, it's tired an' it's torn,
   It looks like it's a-dyin' an' it's hardly been born.

3. Hey, Woody Guthrie, but I know that you know
   All the things that I'm a-sayin' an' a-many times more.
   I'm a-singin' you the song, but I can't sing enough,
   'Cause there's not many men that done the things that you've done.

4. Here's to Cisco an' Sonny an' Leadbelly too,
   An' to all the good people that traveled with you.
   Here's to the hearts and the hands of the men
   That come with the dust and are gone with the wind.

5. I'm a-leavin' tomorrow, but I could leave today,
   Somewhere down the road someday.
   The very last thing that I'd want to do
   Is to say I've been hittin' some hard travelin' too.

Dink's Song

Traditional, arranged by Bob Dylan

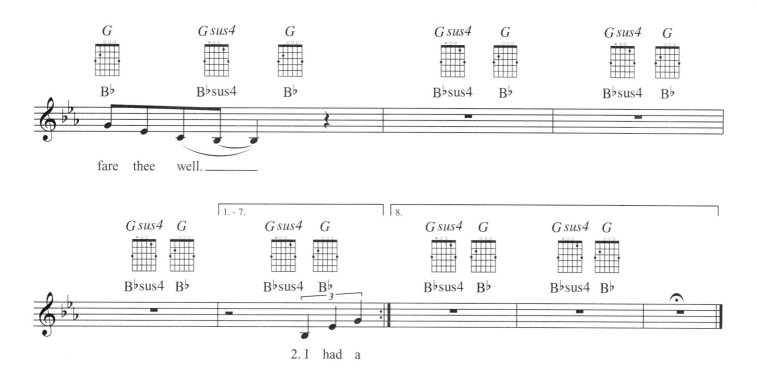

fare thee well. _____

2. I had a

Additional lyrics

2. I had a man
   Who was long and tall,
   Moved his body
   Like a cannonball.
   Fare thee well, my honey,
   Fare thee well.

3. 'Member one evening
   Was drizzling rain,
   And 'round my heart
   I felt an aching pain.
   Fare thee well, my honey,
   Fare thee well.

4. Once I wore
   My apron low,
   Couldn't keep you
   Away from my door.
   Fare thee well, my honey,
   Fare thee well.

5. Now my apron
   Is up to my chin,
   You pass my door
   But you never come in.
   Fare thee well, my honey,
   Fare thee well.

6. Oh, mighty river
   Runs muddy and wild,
   Can't care the bloody
   For my unborn child.
   Fare thee well, my honey,
   Fare thee well.

7. Number 9 train
   Won't do no harm.
   Number 9 train,
   Take my poor baby home.
   Fare thee well, my honey,
   Fare thee well.

8. Fastest man
   I ever saw,
   Skipped Missouri
   On the way to Arkansas.
   Fare thee well, my honey,
   Fare thee well.

I Was Young When I Left Home

Words and Music by Bob Dylan

Additional lyrics

2. It was just the other day,
   I was bringing home my pay
   When I met an old friend I used to know.

3. Said your mother's dead and gone,
   Baby sister's all gone wrong
   And your daddy needs you home right away.

4. Not a shirt on my back,
   Not a penny on my name,
   Well I can't go home thisaway.
   Thisaway, Lord, Lord, Lord.
   And I can't go home thisaway.

5. If you miss the train I'm on,
   Count the days I'm gone.
   You will hear that whistle blow a hundred miles.
   A hundred miles, honey baby. Lord, Lord, Lord.
   And you'll hear that whistle blow a hundred miles.

6. I'm playing on a track,
   Ma would come and whoop me back
   On them trestles down by old Jim McKay's.

7. When I pay the debt I owe
   To the commissary store,
   I will pawn my watch and chain and go home.
   Go home, Lord Lord Lord.
   I will pawn my watch and chain and go home.

8. Used to tell Ma sometimes
   When I see them riding blinds,
   Gonna make me a home out in the wind.
   In the wind, Lord in the wind.
   Make me a home out in the wind.

9. I don't like it in the wind,
   Wanna go back home again,
   But I can't go home thisaway.
   Thisaway, Lord Lord Lord.
   And I can't go home thisaway.

10. I was young when I left home
    And I been all rambling 'round.
    And I never wrote a letter to my home.
    To my home, Lord Lord Lord.
    And I never wrote a letter to my home.

Don't Think Twice, It's All Right

Words and Music by Bob Dylan

16

2.

| G | D7 | G | D | Em |

right. (3. It) ain't no use ___ in call-in' out my name, gal ___
4. I'm walk-in' down ___ that long, lone-some road, babe ___

| C | G | D7 | G | D |

Like you nev – er did be – fore It ain't no use_ in call-in' out my
Where I'm bound, I can't_ tell But good – bye's too good a

| Em | A7 | D | D7 |

name, gal ___ I can't hear you an – y more I'm a –
word, gal ___ So I'll just say fare thee well I ain't

| G | G7 | C | A7 |

think- in' and a – won-d'rin' all the way down the road I once loved a wom- an, _____
say- in' you treat- ed me un – kind You could have done bet – ter _____

| G | Em | C |

_____ a child I'm told I give her my heart but she want- ed my soul.
_____ but I don't mind You just kind- a wast- ed my pre – cious time.

1. **2.**

| G | D7 | G | D7 | G |

But don't think twice, It's all { right 3. It
But don't think twice, It's all { right.

Man of Constant Sorrow

Traditional, arranged by Bob Dylan

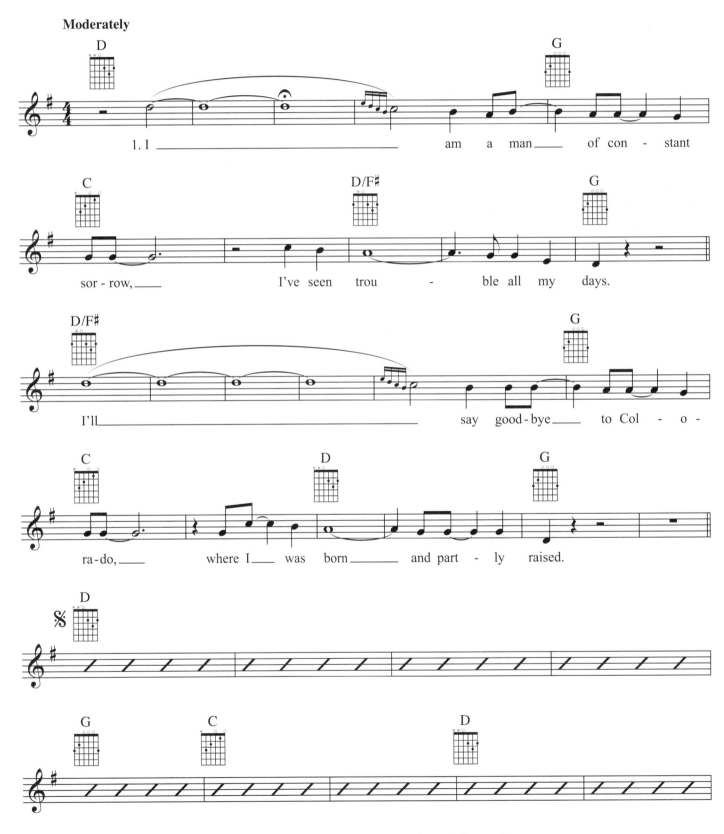

Additional lyrics

2. Through this open world I'm a-bound to ramble,
   Through ice and snow, sleet and rain.
   I'm a-bound to ride that mornin' railroad,
   Perhaps I'll die upon that train.

4. I'm a-goin' back to Colorado,
   The place that I've started from.
   If I'd knowed how bad you'd treat me,
   Babe, I never would have come.

Blowin' in the Wind

Words and Music by Bob Dylan

Masters of War
Words and Music by Bob Dylan

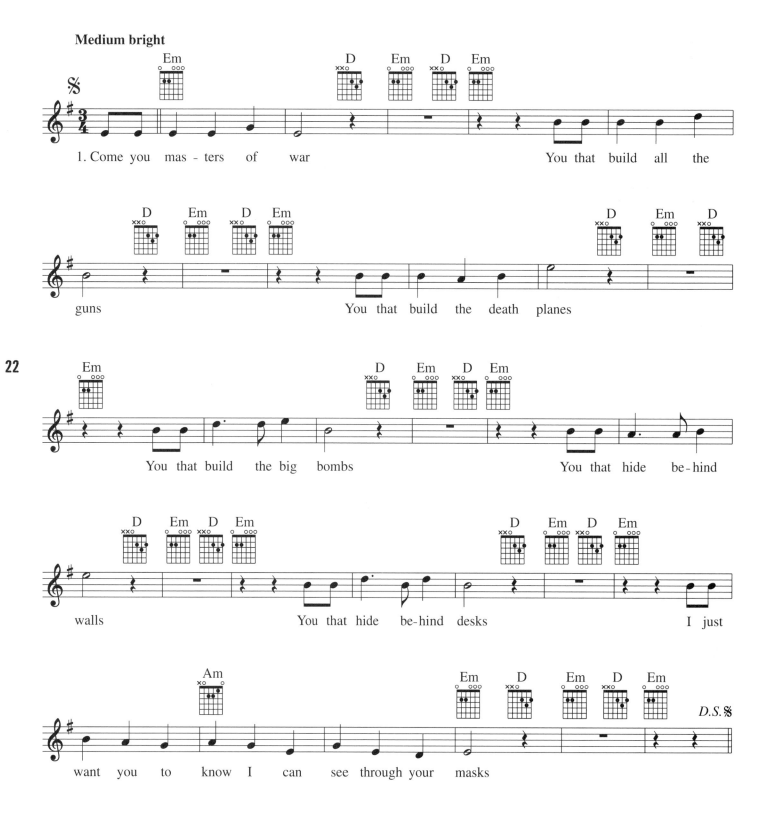

2. You that never done nothin'
   But build to destroy
   You play with my world
   Like it's your little toy
   You put a gun in my hand
   And you hide from my eyes
   And you turn and run farther
   When the fast bullets fly

3. Like Judas of old
   You lie and deceive
   A world war can be won
   You want me to believe
   But I see through your eyes
   And I see through your brain
   Like I see through the water
   That runs down my drain

4. You fasten the triggers
   For the others to fire
   Then you set back and watch
   When the death count gets higher
   You hide in your mansion
   As young people's blood
   Flows out of their bodies
   And is buried in the mud

5. You've thrown the worst fear
   That can ever be hurled
   Fear to bring children
   Into the world
   For threatening my baby
   Unborn and unnamed
   You ain't worth the blood
   That runs in your veins

6. How much do I know
   To talk out of turn
   You might say that I'm young
   You might say I'm unlearned
   But there's one thing I know
   Though I'm younger than you
   Even Jesus would never
   Forgive what you do

7. Let me ask you one question
   Is your money that good
   Will it buy you forgiveness
   Do you think that it could
   I think you will find
   When your death takes its toll
   All the money you made
   Will never buy back your soul

8. And I hope that you die
   And your death'll come soon
   I will follow your casket
   In the pale afternoon
   And I'll watch while you're lowered
   Down to your deathbed
   And I'll stand o'er your grave
   'Til I'm sure that you're dead

23

A Hard Rain's A-Gonna Fall

Words and Music by Bob Dylan

2. Oh, what did you see, my blue-eyed son?
   Oh, what did you see, my darling young one?

   I saw a newborn baby with wild wolves all around it,
   I saw a highway of diamonds with nobody on it,
   I saw a black branch with blood that kept drippin',
   I saw a room full of men with their hammers a-bleedin',
   I saw a white ladder all covered with water,
   I saw ten thousand talkers whose tongues were all broken,

   I saw guns and sharp swords in the hands of young children,
   And it's a hard, and it's a hard, it's a hard, it's a hard,
   And it's a hard rain's a-gonna fall.

3. And what did you hear, my blue-eyed son?
   And what did you hear, my darling young one?

   I heard the sound of a thunder, it roared out a warnin',
   Heard the roar of a wave that could drown the whole world,
   Heard one hundred drummers whose hands were a-blazin',
   Heard ten thousand whisperin' and nobody listenin',
   Heard one person starve, I heard many people laughin',
   Heard the song of a poet who died in the gutter,
   Heard the sound of a clown who cried in the alley,
   And it's a hard, and it's a hard, it's a hard, it's a hard,
   And it's a hard rain's a-gonna fall.

4. Oh, who did you meet, my blue-eyed son?
   Who did you meet, my darling young one?

   I met a young child beside a dead pony,
   I met a white man who walked a black dog,
   I met a young woman whose body was burning,
   I met a young girl, she gave me a rainbow,
   I met one man who was wounded in love,
   I met another man who was wounded with hatred,
   And it's a hard, it's a hard, it's a hard, it's a hard,
   It's a hard rain's a-gonna fall.

5. Oh, what'll you do now, my blue-eyed son?
   Oh, what'll you do now, my darling young one?

   I'm a-goin' back out 'fore the rain starts a-fallin',
   I'll walk to the depths of the deepest black forest,
   Where the people are many and their hands are all empty,
   Where the pellets of poison are flooding their waters,
   Where the home in the valley meets the damp dirty prison,
   Where the executioner's face is always well hidden,
   Where hunger is ugly, where souls are forgotten,
   Where black is the color, where none is the number,
   And I'll tell it and think it and speak it and breathe it,
   And reflect it from the mountain so all souls can see it,
   Then I'll stand on the ocean until I start sinkin',
   But I'll know my song well before I start singin',
   And it's a hard, it's a hard, it's a hard, it's a hard,
   It's a hard rain's a-gonna fall.

When the Ship Comes In

Words and Music by Bob Dylan

2. Oh the fishes will laugh
   As they swim out of the path
   And the seagulls they'll be smiling.
   And the rocks on the sand
   Will proudly stand,
   The hour that the ship comes in.

   And the words that are used
   For to get the ship confused
   Will not be understood as they're spoken.
   For the chains of the sea
   Will have busted in the night
   And will be buried at the bottom of the ocean.

3. A song will lift
   As the mainsail shifts
   And the boat drifts on to the shoreline.
   And the sun will respect
   Every face on the deck,
   The hour that the ship comes in.

   Then the sands will roll
   Out a carpet of gold
   For your weary toes to be a-touchin'.
   And the ship's wise men
   Will remind you once again
   That the whole wide world is watchin'.

4. Oh the foes will rise
   With the sleep still in their eyes
   And they'll jerk from their beds and think they're dreamin'.
   But they'll pinch themselves and squeal
   And know that it's for real,
   The hour when the ship comes in.

   Then they'll raise their hands,
   Sayin' we'll meet all your demands,
   But we'll shout from the bow your days are numbered.
   And like Pharaoh's tribe,
   They'll be drownded in the tide,
   And like Goliath, they'll be conquered.

Chimes of Freedom

Words and Music by Bob Dylan

2. In the city's melted furnace, unexpectedly we watched
   With faces hidden while the walls were tightening
   As the echo of the wedding bells before the blowin' rain
   Dissolved into the bells of the lightning
   Tolling for the rebel, tolling for the rake
   Tolling for the luckless, the abandoned an' forsaked
   Tolling for the outcast, burnin' constantly at stake
   An' we gazed upon the chimes of freedom flashing.

3. Through the mad mystic hammering of the wild ripping hail
   The sky cracked its poems in naked wonder
   That the clinging of the church bells blew far into the breeze
   Leaving only bells of lightning and its thunder
   Striking for the gentle, striking for the kind
   Striking for the guardians and protectors of the mind
   An' the unpawned painter behind beyond his rightful time
   An' we gazed upon the chimes of freedom flashing.

4. Through the wild cathedral evening the rain unraveled tales
   For the disrobed faceless forms of no position
   Tolling for the tongues with no place to bring their thoughts
   All down in taken-for-granted situations
   Tolling for the deaf an' blind, tolling for the mute
   Tolling for the mistreated, mateless mother, the mistitled prostitute
   For the misdemeanor outlaw, chased an' cheated by pursuit
   An' we gazed upon the chimes of freedom flashing.

5. Even though a cloud's white curtain in a far-off corner flashed
   An' the hypnotic splattered mist was slowly lifting
   Electric light still struck like arrows, fired but for the ones
   Condemned to drift or else be kept from drifting
   Tolling for the searching ones, on their speechless, seeking trail
   For the lonesome-hearted lovers with too personal a tale
   An' for each unharmful, gentle soul misplaced inside a jail
   An' we gazed upon the chimes of freedom flashing.

6. Starry-eyed an' laughing as I recall when we were caught
   Trapped by no track of hours for they hanged suspended
   As we listened one last time an' we watched with one last look
   Spellbound an' swallowed 'til the tolling ended
   Tolling for the aching ones whose wounds cannot be nursed
   For the countless confused, accused, misused, strung-out ones an' worse
   An' for every hung-up person in the whole wide universe
   An' we gazed upon the chimes of freedom flashing.

Mr. Tambourine Man

Words and Music by Bob Dylan

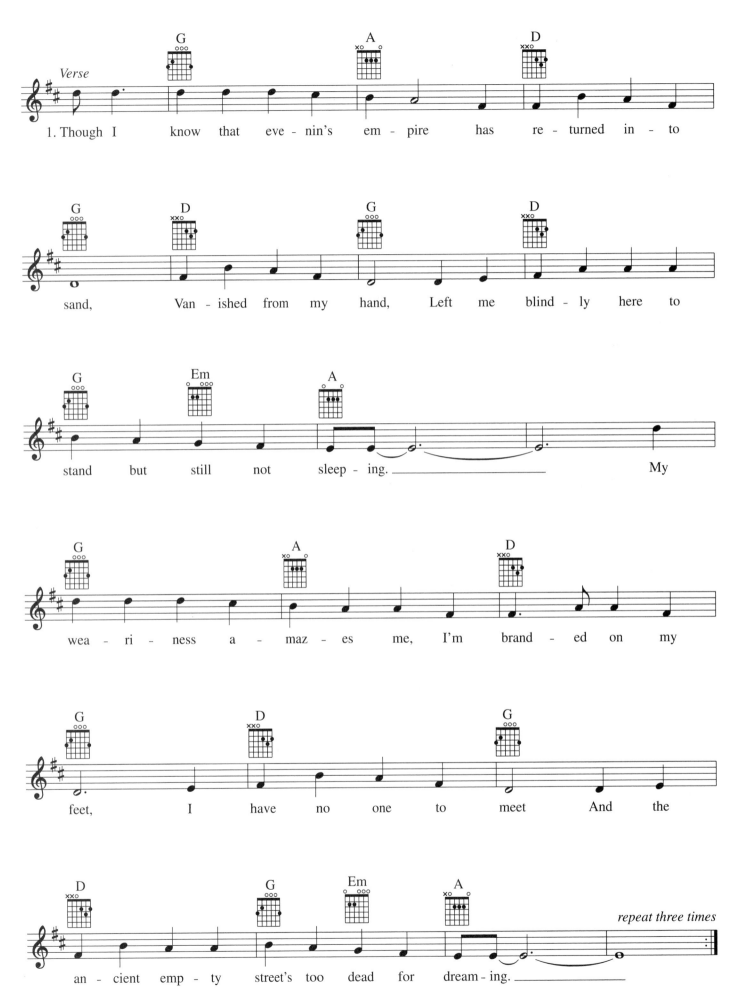

2. Take me on a trip upon your magic swirlin' ship,
   My senses have been stripped, my hands can't feel to grip,
   My toes too numb to step, wait only for my boot heels
   To be wanderin'.
   I'm ready to go anywhere, I'm ready for to fade
   Into my own parade, cast your dancing spell my way,
   I promise to go under it.

   Refrain

3. Though you might hear laughin', spinnin', swingin' madly across the sun,
   It's not aimed at anyone, it's just escapin' on the run
   And but for the sky there are no fences facin'.
   And if you hear vague traces of skippin' reels of rhyme
   To your tambourine in time, it's just a ragged clown behind,
   I wouldn't pay it any mind, it's just a shadow you're
   Seein' that he's chasing.

   Refrain

4. Then take me disappearin' through the smoke rings of my mind,
   Down the foggy ruins of time, far past the frozen leaves,
   The haunted, frightened trees, out to the windy beach,
   Far from the twisted reach of crazy sorrow.
   Yes, to dance beneath the diamond sky with one hand waving free,
   Silhouetted by the sea, circled by the circus sands,
   With all memory and fate driven deep beneath the waves,
   Let me forget about today until tomorrow.

   Refrain

33

It's All Over Now, Baby Blue

Words and Music by Bob Dylan

Medium slow

You must leave now, take what you need, you think will last. But what-

ev - er you wish to keep, you bet - ter grab it fast.

Yon - der stands your or - phan, with his gun,

Cry - ing like a fire in the sun. Look out the

saints are com - in' through And it's all o - ver

now, Ba - by Blue.

Additional lyrics

2. The highway is for gamblers, better use your sense.
Take what you have gathered from coincidence.
The empty-handed painter from your streets
Is drawing crazy patterns on your sheets.
This sky, too, is folding under you
And it's all over now, Baby Blue.

3. All your seasick sailors, they are rowing home.
All your reindeer armies, are all going home.
The lover who just walked out your door
Has taken all his blankets from the floor.
The carpet, too, is moving under you
And it's all over now, Baby Blue.

4. Leave your stepping stones behind, something calls for you.
Forget the dead you've left, they will not follow you.
The vagabond who's rapping at your door
Is standing in the clothes that you once wore.
Strike another match, go start anew
And it's all over now, Baby Blue.

She Belongs to Me

Words and Music by Bob Dylan

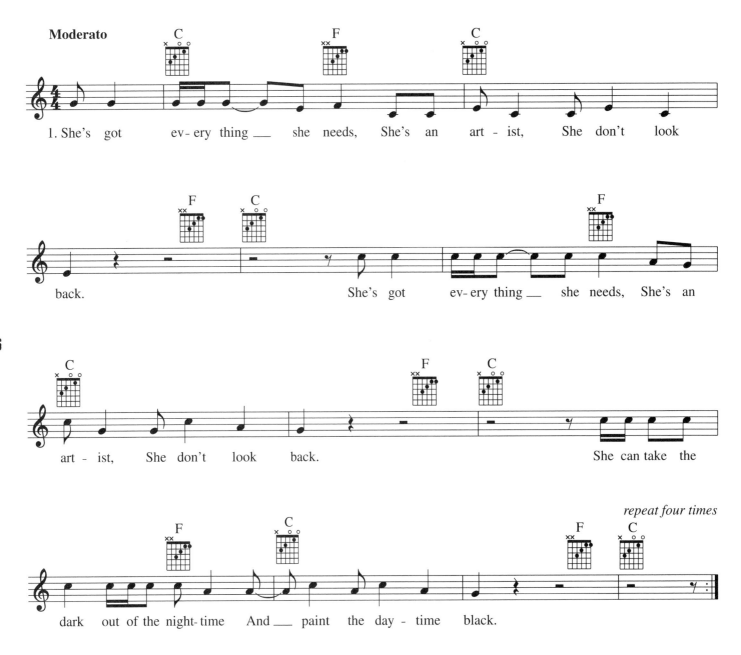

2. You will start out standing
   Proud to steal her anything she sees.
   You will start out standing
   Proud to steal her anything she sees.
   But you will wind up peeking through her keyhole
   Down upon your knees.

3. She never stumbles,
   She's got no place to fall.
   She never stumbles,
   She's got no place to fall.
   She's nobody's child,
   The Law can't touch her at all.

4. She wears an Egyptian ring
   That sparkles before she speaks.
   She wears an Egyptian ring
   That sparkles before she speaks.
   She's a hypnotist collector,
   You are a walking antique.

5. Bow down to her on Sunday,
   Salute her when her birthday comes.
   Bow down to her on Sunday,
   Salute her when her birthday comes.
   For Halloween give her a trumpet
   And for Christmas, buy her a drum.

Maggie's Farm

Words and Music by Bob Dylan

2. I ain't gonna work for Maggie's brother no more.
   No, I ain't gonna work for Maggie's brother no more.
   Well, he hands you a nickel,
   He hands you a dime,
   He asks you with a grin
   If you're havin' a good time,
   Then he fines you every time you slam the door.
   I ain't gonna work for Maggie's brother no more.

3. I ain't gonna work for Maggie's pa no more.
   No, I ain't gonna work for Maggie's pa no more.
   Well, he puts his cigar
   Out in your face just for kicks.
   His bedroom window
   It is made out of bricks.
   The National Guard stands around his door.
   Ah, I ain't gonna work for Maggie's pa no more.

4. I ain't gonna work for Maggie's ma no more.
   No, I ain't gonna work for Maggie's ma no more.
   Well, she talks to all the servants
   About man and God and law.
   Everybody says
   She's the brains behind pa.
   She's sixty-eight, but she says she's twenty-four.
   I ain't gonna work for Maggie's ma no more.

5. I ain't gonna work on Maggie's farm no more.
   No, I ain't gonna work on Maggie's farm no more.
   Well, I try my best
   To be just like I am,
   But everybody wants you
   To be just like them.
   They sing while you slave and I just get bored.
   I ain't gonna work on Maggie's farm no more.

Tombstone Blues

Words and Music by Bob Dylan

bald wig for Jack the Rip - per _____ who sits at the

head of the cham - ber of com - merce _____ Ma - ma's in the

Chorus

fac - 'try _____ She ain't got no shoes _____ Dad - dy's in the

al - ley He's look - in' for the fuse, I'm in the streets With the

repeat five times

tomb - stone blues _____

2. The hysterical bride in the penny arcade
   Screaming she moans, "I've just been made"
   Then sends out for the doctor who pulls down the shade
   Says, "My advice is to not let the boys in"

   Now the medicine man comes and he shuffles inside
   He walks with a swagger and he says to the bride
   "Stop all this weeping, swallow your pride
   You will not die, it's not poison"

   Chorus

3. Well, John the Baptist after torturing a thief
   Looks up at his hero the Commander-in-Chief
   Saying, "Tell me great hero, but please make it brief
   Is there a hole for me to get sick in?"

   The Commander-in-Chief answers him while chasing a fly
   Saying, "Death to all those who would whimper and cry"
   And dropping a bar bell he points to the sky
   Saving, "The sun's not yellow it's chicken"

   Chorus

4. The king of the Philistines his soldiers to save
   Put jawbones on their tombstones and flatters their graves
   Puts the pied pipers in prison and fattens the slaves
   Then sends them out to the jungle

   Gypsy Davey with a blowtorch he burns out their camps
   With his faithful slave Pedro behind him he tramps
   With a fantastic collection of stamps
   To win friends and influence his uncle

   Chorus

5. The geometry of innocence flesh on the bone
   Causes Galileo's math book to get thrown
   At Delilah who sits worthlessly alone
   But the tears on her cheeks are from laughter

   Now I wish I could give Brother Bill his great thrill
   I would set him in chains at the top of the hill
   Then send out for some pillars and Cecil B. DeMille
   He could die happily ever after

   Chorus

6. Where Ma Raney and Beethoven once unwrapped their bed roll
   Tuba players now rehearse around the flagpole
   And the National Bank at a profit sells road maps for the soul
   To the old folks home and the college

   Now I wish I could write you a melody so plain
   That could hold you dear lady from going insane
   That could ease you and cool you and cease the pain
   Of your useless and pointless knowledge

   Chorus

42

It Takes a Lot to Laugh, It Takes a Train to Cry

Words and Music by Bob Dylan

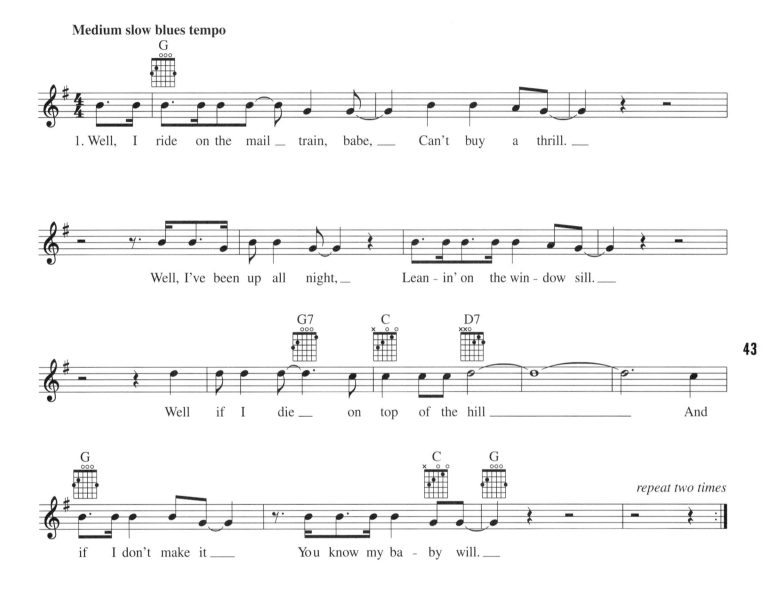

Medium slow blues tempo

1. Well, I ride on the mail train, babe, Can't buy a thrill.

Well, I've been up all night, Lean - in' on the win - dow sill.

Well if I die on top of the hill And

if I don't make it You know my ba - by will.

repeat two times

Additional lyrics

2. Don't the moon look good, mama,
   Shinin' through the trees?
   Don't the brakeman look good, mama,
   Flagging down the "Double E"?
   Don't the sun look good
   Goin' down over the sea?
   Don't my gal look fine
   When she's comin' after me?

3. Now the wintertime is coming,
   The windows are filled with frost.
   I went to tell everybody,
   But I could not get across.
   Well, I wanna be your lover, baby,
   I don't wanna be your boss.
   Don't say I never warned you
   When your train gets lost.

Just Like Tom Thumb's Blues

Words and Music by Bob Dylan

2. Now if you see Saint Annie
   Please tell her thanks a lot
   I cannot move
   My fingers are all in a knot
   I don't have the strength
   To get up and take another shot
   And my best friend, my doctor
   Won't even say what it is I've got

3. Sweet Melinda
   The peasants call her the goddess of gloom
   She speaks good English
   And she invites you up into her room
   And you're so kind
   And careful not to go to her too soon
   And she takes your voice
   And leaves you howling at the moon

4. Up on Housing Project Hill
   It's either fortune or fame
   You must pick up one or the other
   Though neither of them are to be what they claim
   If you're lookin' to get silly
   You better go back to from where you came
   Because the cops don't need you
   And man they expect the same

5. Now all the authorities
   They just stand around and boast
   How they blackmailed the sergeant-at-arms
   Into leaving his post
   And picking up Angel who
   Just arrived here from the coast
   Who looked so fine at first
   But left looking just like a ghost

6. I started out on burgundy
   But soon hit the harder stuff
   Everybody said they'd stand behind me
   When the game got rough
   But the joke was on me
   There was nobody even there to call my bluff
   I'm going back to New York City
   I do believe I've had enough

Desolation Row

Words and Music by Bob Dylan

2. Cinderella, she seems so easy,
   "It takes one to know one," she smiles,
   And puts her hands in her back pockets
   Bette Davis style
   And in comes Romeo, he's moaning,
   "You Belong to Me I Believe"
   And someone says," You're in the wrong place, my friend
   You better leave."
   And the only sound that's left
   After the ambulances go
   Is Cinderella sweeping up
   On Desolation Row

3. Now the moon is almost hidden
   The stars are beginning to hide
   The fortunetelling lady
   Has even taken all her things inside
   All except for Cain and Abel
   And the hunchback of Notre Dame
   Everybody is making love
   Or else expecting rain
   And the Good Samaritan, he's dressing
   He's getting ready for the show
   He's going to the carnival tonight
   On Desolation Row

4. Now Ophelia, she's 'neath the window
   For her I feel so afraid
   On her twenty-second birthday
   She already is an old maid
   To her, death is quite romantic
   She wears an iron vest
   Her profession's her religion
   Her sin is her lifelessness
   And though her eyes are fixed upon
   Noah's great rainbow
   She spends her time peeking
   Into Desolation Row

5. Einstein, disguised as Robin Hood
   With his memories in a trunk
   Passed this way an hour ago
   With his friend, a jealous monk
   He looked so immaculately frightful
   As he bummed a cigarette
   Then he went off sniffing drainpipes
   And reciting the alphabet
   Now you would not think to look at him
   But he was famous long ago
   For playing the electric violin
   On Desolation Row

6. Dr. Filth, he keeps his world
   Inside of a leather cup
   But all his sexless patients
   They're trying to blow it up
   Now his nurse, some local loser
   She's in charge of the cyanide hole
   And she also keeps the cards that read
   "Have Mercy on His Soul."
   They all play on penny whistles
   You can hear them blow
   If you lean your head out far enough
   From Desolation Row

7. Across the street they've nailed the curtains
   They're getting ready for the feast
   The Phantom of the Opera
   A perfect image of a priest
   They're spoonfeeding Casanova
   To get him to feel more assured
   Then they'll kill him with self-confidence
   After poisoning him with words
   And the Phantom's shouting to skinny girls
   "Get Outa Here If You Don't Know
   Casanova is just being punished for going
   To Desolation Row"

8. Now at midnight all the agents
   And the superhuman crew
   Come out and round up everyone
   That knows more than they do
   Then they bring them to the factory
   Where the heart-attack machine
   Is strapped across their shoulders
   And then the kerosene
   Is brought down from the castles
   By insurance men who go
   Check to see that nobody is escaping
   To Desolation Row

9. Praise be to Nero's Neptune
   The Titanic sails at dawn
   And everybody's shouting
   "Which Side Are You On?"
   And Ezra Pound and T. S. Eliot
   Fighting in the captain's tower
   While calypso singers laugh at them
   And fishermen hold flowers
   Between the windows of the sea
   Where lovely mermaids flow
   And nobody has to think too much
   About Desolation Row

10. Yes, I received your letter yesterday
    (About the time the door knob broke)
    When you asked how I was doing
    Was that some kind of joke?
    All these people that you mention
    Yes, I know them, they're quite lame
    I had to rearrange their faces
    And give them all another name
    Right now I can't read too good
    Don't send me no more letters no
    Not unless you mail them
    From Desolation Row

47

Highway 61 Revisited

Words and Music by Bob Dylan

2. Well Georgia Sam he had a bloody nose
   Welfare Department they wouldn't give him no clothes
   He asked poor Howard where can I go
   Howard said there's only one place I know
   Sam said tell me quick man I got to run
   Ol' Howard just pointed with his gun
   And said that way down on Highway 61.

3. Well Mack the Finger said to Louie the King
   I got forty red white and blue shoe strings
   And a thousand telephones that don't ring
   Do you know where I can get rid of these things
   And Louie the King said let me think for a minute son
   And he said yes I think it can be easily done
   Just take everything down to Highway 61.

4. Now the fifth daughter on the twelfth night
   Told the first father that things weren't right
   My complexion she said is much too white
   He said come here and step into the light he says hmm you're right
   Let me tell the second mother this has been done
   But the second mother was with the seventh son
   And they were both out on Highway 61.

5. Now the rovin' gambler he was very bored
   He was tryin' to create a next world war
   He found a promoter who nearly fell off the floor
   He said I never engaged in this kind of thing before
   But yes I think it can be very easily done
   We'll just put some bleachers out in the sun
   And have it on Highway 61.

Leopard-skin Pill-box Hat

Words and Music by Bob Dylan

2. Well, you look so pretty in it
   Honey, can I jump on it sometime?
   Yes, I just wanna see
   If it's really that expensive kind
   You know it balances on your head
   Just like a mattress balances
   On a bottle of wine
   Your brand new leopard-skin pill-box hat

3. Well, if you wanna see the sun rise
   Honey, I know where
   We'll go out and see it sometime
   We'll both just sit there and stare
   Me with my belt
   Wrapped around my head
   And you just sittin' there
   In your brand new leopard-skin pill-box hat

4. Well, I asked the doctor if I could see you
   It's bad for your health, he said
   Yes, I disobeyed his orders
   I came to see you
   But I found him there instead
   You know, I don't mind him cheatin' on me
   But I sure wish he'd take that off his head
   Your brand new leopard-skin pill-box hat

5. Well, I see you got a new boyfriend
   You know, I never seen him before
   Well, I saw him
   Makin' love to you
   You forgot to close the garage door
   You might think he loves you for your money
   But I know what he really loves you for
   It's your brand new leopard-skin pill-box hat

Visions of Johanna

Words and Music by Bob Dylan

53

Stuck Inside of Mobile
with the Memphis Blues Again

Words and Music by Bob Dylan

Chorus

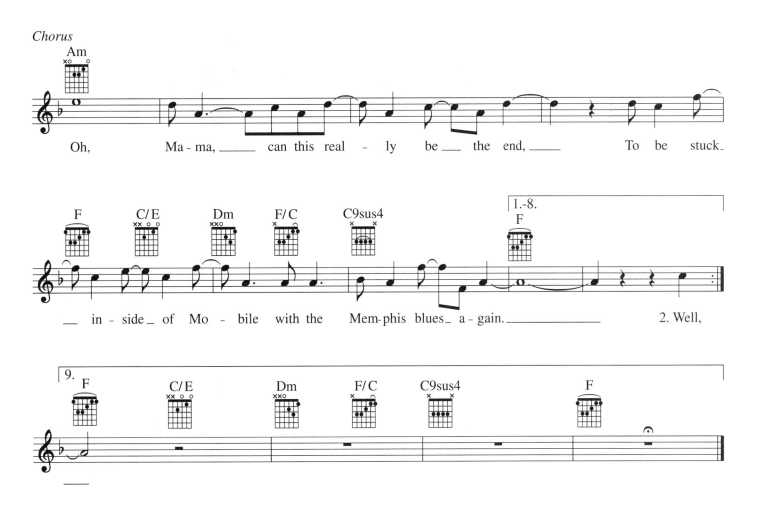

Oh, Ma-ma, _____ can this real - ly be _ the end, _____ To be stuck_

_ in - side _ of Mo - bile with the Mem-phis blues_ a - gain. _____ 2. Well,

1.-8.

9.

Additional lyrics

2. Well, Shakespeare, he's in the alley
With his pointed shoes and his bells,
Speaking to some French girl,
Who says she knows me well.
And I would send a message
To find out if she's talked,
But the post office has been stolen
And the mailbox is locked.

Chorus

3. Mona tried to tell me
To stay away from the train line.
She said that all the railroad men
Just drink up your blood like wine.
An' I said, "Oh, I didn't know that,
But then again, there's only one I've met
An' he just smoked my eyelids
An' punched my cigarette."

Chorus

4. Grandpa died last week
And now he's buried in the rocks,
But everybody still talks about
How badly they were shocked.
But me, I expected it to happen,
I knew he'd lost control
When he built a fire on Main Street
And shot it full of holes.

Chorus

5. Now the senator came down here
Showing ev'ryone his gun,
Handing out free tickets
To the wedding of his son.
An' me, I nearly got busted
An' wouldn't it be my luck
To get caught without a ticket
And be discovered beneath a truck.

Chorus

6. Now the preacher looked so baffled
When I asked him why he dressed
With twenty pounds of headlines
Stapled to his chest.
But he cursed me when I proved it to him,
Then I whispered, "Not even you can hide.
You see, you're just like me,
I hope you're satisfied."

Chorus

7. Now the rainman gave me two cures,
Then he said, "Jump right in."
The one was Texas medicine,
The other was just railroad gin.
An' like a fool I mixed them
An' it strangled up my mind,
An' now people just get uglier
An' I have no sense of time.

Chorus

8. When Ruthie says come see her
In her honky-tonk lagoon,
Where I can watch her waltz for free
'Neath her Panamanian moon.
An' I say, "Aw come on now,
You must know about my debutante."
An' she says, "Your debutante just knows what you need
But I know what you want."

Chorus

9. Now the bricks lay on Grand Street
Where the neon madmen climb.
They all fall there so perfectly,
It all seems so well timed.
An' here I sit so patiently
Waiting to find out what price
You have to pay to get out of
Going through all these things twice.

Chorus

Ballad of a Thin Man

Words and Music by Bob Dylan

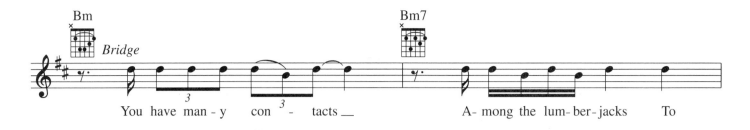

Bridge

You have man - y con - tacts ___ A- mong the lum- ber- jacks To

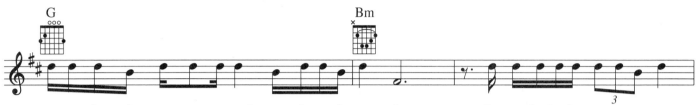

get you facts when some-one at-tacks your im-ag-i - na - tion But no-bod-y has an- y res-pect

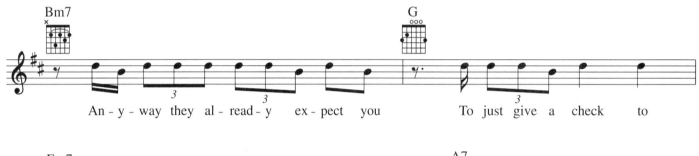

An - y - way they al - read-y ex - pect you To just give a check to

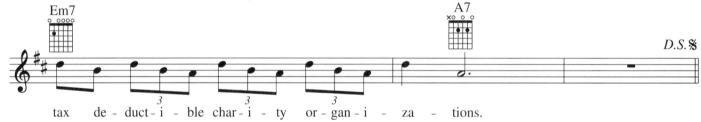

tax de- duct- i - ble char- i - ty or- gan- i - za - tions.

D.S. 𝄋

2. You raise up your head
   And you ask, "Is this where it is?"
   And somebody points to you and says,
   "It's his."
   And you say, "What's mine?"
   And somebody else says, "Where what is?"
   And you say, "Oh my God
   Am I here all alone?"

   Because something is happening here
   But you don't know what it is
   Do you, Mister Jones?

3. You hand in your ticket
   And you go watch the geek
   Who immediately walks up to you
   When he hears you speak.
   And says, "How does it feel
   To be such a freak?"
   And you say, "Impossible,"
   As he hands you a bone

   Because something is happening here
   But you don't know what it is
   Do you, Mister Jones?

   Bridge:
   You have many contacts
   Among the lumberjacks
   To get you facts
   When someone attacks your imagination
   But nobody has any respect
   Anyway they already expect you
   To just give a check
   To tax-deductible charity organizations

4. You've been with the professors
   And they've all liked your looks
   With great lawyers you have
   Discussed lepers and crooks
   You've been through all of
   F. Scott Fitzgerald's books
   You're very well read
   It's well known

   Because something is happening here
   But you don't know what it is
   Do you, Mister Jones?

5. Well, the sword swallower, he comes up to you
   And then he kneels
   He crosses himself
   And then he clicks his high heels
   And without further notice
   He asks you how it feels
   And he says, "Here is your throat back
   Thanks for the loan"

   Because something is happening here
   But you don't know what it is
   Do you, Mister Jones?

6. Now you see this one-eyed midget
   Shouting the word "NOW"
   And you say, "For what reason?"
   And he says, "How?"
   And you say, "What does this mean?"
   And he screams back, "You're a cow
   Give me some milk
   Or else go home"

   Because something is happening here
   But you don't know what it is
   Do you, Mister Jones?

7. Well, you walk into the room
   Like a camel and then you frown
   You put your eyes in your pocket
   And your nose on the ground
   There ought to be a law
   Against you comin' around
   You should be made
   To wear earphones

   Because something is happening here
   But you don't know what it is
   Do you, Mister Jones?

Like a Rolling Stone

Words and Music by Bob Dylan

hang - in' out ___ Now you don't talk so loud _____

Now you don't seem so proud _____ A - bout hav - ing to be

scroung - ing for your next meal. _____

Refrain

How does it feel How does it feel

To be with-out a home

Like a com- plete un - known Like a roll - ing stone?

Tag

fourth time to Tag

2. You've gone to the finest school all right, Miss Lonely
   But you know you only used to get juiced in it
   And nobody has ever taught you how to live on the street
   And now you find out you're gonna have to get used to it
   You said you'd never compromise
   With the mystery tramp, but now you realize
   He's not selling any alibis
   As you stare into the vacuum of his eyes
   And ask him do you want to make a deal?

   Refrain

3. You never turned around to see the frowns on the jugglers and the clowns
   When they all come down and did tricks for you
   You never understood that it ain't no good
   You shouldn't let other people get your kicks for you
   You used to ride on the chrome horse with your diplomat
   Who carried on his shoulder a Siamese cat
   Ain't it hard when you discover that
   He really wasn't where it's at
   After he took from you everything he could steal.

   Refrain

4. Princess on the steeple and all the pretty people
   They're drinkin', thinkin' that they got it made
   Exchanging all kinds of precious gifts and things
   But you'd better lift your diamond ring, you'd better pawn it babe
   You used to be so amused
   At Napoleon in rags and the language that he used
   Go to him now, he calls you, you can't refuse
   When you got nothing, you got nothing to lose
   You're invisible now, you got no secrets to conceal.

   Refrain